THIS FOREX TRADING JOURNAL

Belongs To

_____

Copyright © Note Lovers
www.NoteLovers.com

Trade #　　　　　　Entry Date　　　　　　Time Open　　　　　　Time Closed

FX Pair	Buy / Sell	Trade Size	Entry Price	Target Price	Stop Loss	Exit Price

Reason for Trade Entry:
Strategy:
Trade Result Remarks:
Notes:

Trade #　　　　　　Entry Date　　　　　　Time Open　　　　　　Time Closed

FX Pair	Buy / Sell	Trade Size	Entry Price	Target Price	Stop Loss	Exit Price

Reason for Trade Entry:
Strategy:
Trade Result Remarks:
Notes:

Trade #   Entry Date   Time Open   Time Closed

FX Pair	Buy / Sell	Trade Size	Entry Price	Target Price	Stop Loss	Exit Price

Reason for Trade Entry:
Strategy:
Trade Result Remarks:
Notes:

Trade #   Entry Date   Time Open   Time Closed

FX Pair	Buy / Sell	Trade Size	Entry Price	Target Price	Stop Loss	Exit Price

Reason for Trade Entry:
Strategy:
Trade Result Remarks:
Notes:

Trade #   Entry Date   Time Open   Time Closed

FX Pair	Buy / Sell	Trade Size	Entry Price	Target Price	Stop Loss	Exit Price

Reason for Trade Entry:
Strategy:
Trade Result Remarks:
Notes:

Trade #   Entry Date   Time Open   Time Closed

FX Pair	Buy / Sell	Trade Size	Entry Price	Target Price	Stop Loss	Exit Price

Reason for Trade Entry:
Strategy:
Trade Result Remarks:
Notes:

Trade #   Entry Date   Time Open   Time Closed

FX Pair	Buy / Sell	Trade Size	Entry Price	Target Price	Stop Loss	Exit Price

Reason for Trade Entry:
Strategy:
Trade Result Remarks:
Notes:

Trade #   Entry Date   Time Open   Time Closed

FX Pair	Buy / Sell	Trade Size	Entry Price	Target Price	Stop Loss	Exit Price

Reason for Trade Entry:
Strategy:
Trade Result Remarks:
Notes:

Trade # **Entry Date** **Time Open** **Time Closed**

FX Pair	Buy / Sell	Trade Size	Entry Price	Target Price	Stop Loss	Exit Price

Reason for Trade Entry:
Strategy:
Trade Result Remarks:
Notes:

Trade # **Entry Date** **Time Open** **Time Closed**

FX Pair	Buy / Sell	Trade Size	Entry Price	Target Price	Stop Loss	Exit Price

Reason for Trade Entry:
Strategy:
Trade Result Remarks:
Notes:

Trade #	Entry Date	Time Open	Time Closed

FX Pair	Buy / Sell	Trade Size	Entry Price	Target Price	Stop Loss	Exit Price

Reason for Trade Entry:
Strategy:
Trade Result Remarks:
Notes:

Trade #	Entry Date	Time Open	Time Closed

FX Pair	Buy / Sell	Trade Size	Entry Price	Target Price	Stop Loss	Exit Price

Reason for Trade Entry:
Strategy:
Trade Result Remarks:
Notes:

Trade #   **Entry Date**   **Time Open**   **Time Closed**

FX Pair	Buy / Sell	Trade Size	Entry Price	Target Price	Stop Loss	Exit Price

Reason for Trade Entry:
Strategy:
Trade Result Remarks:
Notes:

Trade #   **Entry Date**   **Time Open**   **Time Closed**

FX Pair	Buy / Sell	Trade Size	Entry Price	Target Price	Stop Loss	Exit Price

Reason for Trade Entry:
Strategy:
Trade Result Remarks:
Notes:

Trade #   Entry Date   Time Open   Time Closed

FX Pair	Buy / Sell	Trade Size	Entry Price	Target Price	Stop Loss	Exit Price

Reason for Trade Entry:
Strategy:
Trade Result Remarks:
Notes:

Trade #   Entry Date   Time Open   Time Closed

FX Pair	Buy / Sell	Trade Size	Entry Price	Target Price	Stop Loss	Exit Price

Reason for Trade Entry:
Strategy:
Trade Result Remarks:
Notes:

Trade #　　　　　　**Entry Date**　　　　　　**Time Open**　　　　　　**Time Closed**

FX Pair	Buy / Sell	Trade Size	Entry Price	Target Price	Stop Loss	Exit Price

Reason for Trade Entry:
Strategy:
Trade Result Remarks:
Notes:

Trade #　　　　　　**Entry Date**　　　　　　**Time Open**　　　　　　**Time Closed**

FX Pair	Buy / Sell	Trade Size	Entry Price	Target Price	Stop Loss	Exit Price

Reason for Trade Entry:
Strategy:
Trade Result Remarks:
Notes:

Trade #   **Entry Date**   **Time Open**   **Time Closed**

FX Pair	Buy / Sell	Trade Size	Entry Price	Target Price	Stop Loss	Exit Price

Reason for Trade Entry:
Strategy:
Trade Result Remarks:
Notes:

Trade #   **Entry Date**   **Time Open**   **Time Closed**

FX Pair	Buy / Sell	Trade Size	Entry Price	Target Price	Stop Loss	Exit Price

Reason for Trade Entry:
Strategy:
Trade Result Remarks:
Notes:

Trade #   Entry Date   Time Open   Time Closed

FX Pair	Buy / Sell	Trade Size	Entry Price	Target Price	Stop Loss	Exit Price

Reason for Trade Entry:	
Strategy:	
Trade Result Remarks:	
Notes:	

Trade #   Entry Date   Time Open   Time Closed

FX Pair	Buy / Sell	Trade Size	Entry Price	Target Price	Stop Loss	Exit Price

Reason for Trade Entry:	
Strategy:	
Trade Result Remarks:	
Notes:	

Trade #   Entry Date   Time Open   Time Closed

FX Pair	Buy / Sell	Trade Size	Entry Price	Target Price	Stop Loss	Exit Price

Reason for Trade Entry:
Strategy:
Trade Result Remarks:
Notes:

Trade #   Entry Date   Time Open   Time Closed

FX Pair	Buy / Sell	Trade Size	Entry Price	Target Price	Stop Loss	Exit Price

Reason for Trade Entry:
Strategy:
Trade Result Remarks:
Notes:

Trade #   Entry Date   Time Open   Time Closed

FX Pair	Buy / Sell	Trade Size	Entry Price	Target Price	Stop Loss	Exit Price

Reason for Trade Entry:
Strategy:
Trade Result Remarks:
Notes:

Trade #   Entry Date   Time Open   Time Closed

FX Pair	Buy / Sell	Trade Size	Entry Price	Target Price	Stop Loss	Exit Price

Reason for Trade Entry:
Strategy:
Trade Result Remarks:
Notes:

Trade #　　　　Entry Date　　　　Time Open　　　　Time Closed

FX Pair	Buy / Sell	Trade Size	Entry Price	Target Price	Stop Loss	Exit Price

Reason for Trade Entry:
Strategy:
Trade Result Remarks:
Notes:

Trade #　　　　Entry Date　　　　Time Open　　　　Time Closed

FX Pair	Buy / Sell	Trade Size	Entry Price	Target Price	Stop Loss	Exit Price

Reason for Trade Entry:
Strategy:
Trade Result Remarks:
Notes:

Trade #   Entry Date   Time Open   Time Closed

FX Pair	Buy / Sell	Trade Size	Entry Price	Target Price	Stop Loss	Exit Price

Reason for Trade Entry:
Strategy:
Trade Result Remarks:
Notes:

Trade #   Entry Date   Time Open   Time Closed

FX Pair	Buy / Sell	Trade Size	Entry Price	Target Price	Stop Loss	Exit Price

Reason for Trade Entry:
Strategy:
Trade Result Remarks:
Notes:

Trade #　　　　Entry Date　　　　Time Open　　　　Time Closed

FX Pair	Buy / Sell	Trade Size	Entry Price	Target Price	Stop Loss	Exit Price

Reason for Trade Entry:
Strategy:
Trade Result Remarks:
Notes:

Trade #　　　　Entry Date　　　　Time Open　　　　Time Closed

FX Pair	Buy / Sell	Trade Size	Entry Price	Target Price	Stop Loss	Exit Price

Reason for Trade Entry:
Strategy:
Trade Result Remarks:
Notes:

Trade #   Entry Date   Time Open   Time Closed

FX Pair	Buy / Sell	Trade Size	Entry Price	Target Price	Stop Loss	Exit Price

Reason for Trade Entry:
Strategy:
Trade Result Remarks:
Notes:

Trade #   Entry Date   Time Open   Time Closed

FX Pair	Buy / Sell	Trade Size	Entry Price	Target Price	Stop Loss	Exit Price

Reason for Trade Entry:
Strategy:
Trade Result Remarks:
Notes:

Trade #　　　　　Entry Date　　　　　Time Open　　　　　Time Closed

FX Pair	Buy / Sell	Trade Size	Entry Price	Target Price	Stop Loss	Exit Price

Reason for Trade Entry:
Strategy:
Trade Result Remarks:
Notes:

Trade #　　　　　Entry Date　　　　　Time Open　　　　　Time Closed

FX Pair	Buy / Sell	Trade Size	Entry Price	Target Price	Stop Loss	Exit Price

Reason for Trade Entry:
Strategy:
Trade Result Remarks:
Notes:

Trade #   **Entry Date**   **Time Open**   **Time Closed**

FX Pair	Buy / Sell	Trade Size	Entry Price	Target Price	Stop Loss	Exit Price

Reason for Trade Entry:
Strategy:
Trade Result Remarks:
Notes:

Trade #   **Entry Date**   **Time Open**   **Time Closed**

FX Pair	Buy / Sell	Trade Size	Entry Price	Target Price	Stop Loss	Exit Price

Reason for Trade Entry:
Strategy:
Trade Result Remarks:
Notes:

Trade #   Entry Date   Time Open   Time Closed

FX Pair	Buy / Sell	Trade Size	Entry Price	Target Price	Stop Loss	Exit Price

Reason for Trade Entry:
Strategy:
Trade Result Remarks:
Notes:

Trade #   Entry Date   Time Open   Time Closed

FX Pair	Buy / Sell	Trade Size	Entry Price	Target Price	Stop Loss	Exit Price

Reason for Trade Entry:
Strategy:
Trade Result Remarks:
Notes:

Trade #   Entry Date   Time Open   Time Closed

FX Pair	Buy / Sell	Trade Size	Entry Price	Target Price	Stop Loss	Exit Price

Reason for Trade Entry:
Strategy:
Trade Result Remarks:
Notes:

Trade #   Entry Date   Time Open   Time Closed

FX Pair	Buy / Sell	Trade Size	Entry Price	Target Price	Stop Loss	Exit Price

Reason for Trade Entry:
Strategy:
Trade Result Remarks:
Notes:

Trade #   Entry Date   Time Open   Time Closed

FX Pair	Buy / Sell	Trade Size	Entry Price	Target Price	Stop Loss	Exit Price

Reason for Trade Entry:
Strategy:
Trade Result Remarks:
Notes:

Trade #   Entry Date   Time Open   Time Closed

FX Pair	Buy / Sell	Trade Size	Entry Price	Target Price	Stop Loss	Exit Price

Reason for Trade Entry:
Strategy:
Trade Result Remarks:
Notes:

Trade #   Entry Date   Time Open   Time Closed

FX Pair	Buy / Sell	Trade Size	Entry Price	Target Price	Stop Loss	Exit Price

Reason for Trade Entry:
Strategy:
Trade Result Remarks:
Notes:

Trade #   Entry Date   Time Open   Time Closed

FX Pair	Buy / Sell	Trade Size	Entry Price	Target Price	Stop Loss	Exit Price

Reason for Trade Entry:
Strategy:
Trade Result Remarks:
Notes:

Trade #   Entry Date   Time Open   Time Closed

FX Pair	Buy / Sell	Trade Size	Entry Price	Target Price	Stop Loss	Exit Price

Reason for Trade Entry:
Strategy:
Trade Result Remarks:
Notes:

Trade #   Entry Date   Time Open   Time Closed

FX Pair	Buy / Sell	Trade Size	Entry Price	Target Price	Stop Loss	Exit Price

Reason for Trade Entry:
Strategy:
Trade Result Remarks:
Notes:

Trade #   Entry Date   Time Open   Time Closed

FX Pair	Buy / Sell	Trade Size	Entry Price	Target Price	Stop Loss	Exit Price

Reason for Trade Entry:
Strategy:
Trade Result Remarks:
Notes:

Trade #   Entry Date   Time Open   Time Closed

FX Pair	Buy / Sell	Trade Size	Entry Price	Target Price	Stop Loss	Exit Price

Reason for Trade Entry:
Strategy:
Trade Result Remarks:
Notes:

Trade # **Entry Date** **Time Open** **Time Closed**

FX Pair	Buy / Sell	Trade Size	Entry Price	Target Price	Stop Loss	Exit Price

Reason for Trade Entry:
Strategy:
Trade Result Remarks:
Notes:

Trade # **Entry Date** **Time Open** **Time Closed**

FX Pair	Buy / Sell	Trade Size	Entry Price	Target Price	Stop Loss	Exit Price

Reason for Trade Entry:
Strategy:
Trade Result Remarks:
Notes:

Trade #   **Entry Date**   **Time Open**   **Time Closed**

FX Pair	Buy / Sell	Trade Size	Entry Price	Target Price	Stop Loss	Exit Price

Reason for Trade Entry:
Strategy:
Trade Result Remarks:
Notes:

Trade #   **Entry Date**   **Time Open**   **Time Closed**

FX Pair	Buy / Sell	Trade Size	Entry Price	Target Price	Stop Loss	Exit Price

Reason for Trade Entry:
Strategy:
Trade Result Remarks:
Notes:

Trade #   Entry Date   Time Open   Time Closed

FX Pair	Buy / Sell	Trade Size	Entry Price	Target Price	Stop Loss	Exit Price

Reason for Trade Entry:
Strategy:
Trade Result Remarks:
Notes:

Trade #   Entry Date   Time Open   Time Closed

FX Pair	Buy / Sell	Trade Size	Entry Price	Target Price	Stop Loss	Exit Price

Reason for Trade Entry:
Strategy:
Trade Result Remarks:
Notes:

Trade #   Entry Date   Time Open   Time Closed

FX Pair	Buy / Sell	Trade Size	Entry Price	Target Price	Stop Loss	Exit Price

Reason for Trade Entry:
Strategy:
Trade Result Remarks:
Notes:

Trade #   Entry Date   Time Open   Time Closed

FX Pair	Buy / Sell	Trade Size	Entry Price	Target Price	Stop Loss	Exit Price

Reason for Trade Entry:
Strategy:
Trade Result Remarks:
Notes:

Trade #   Entry Date   Time Open   Time Closed

FX Pair	Buy / Sell	Trade Size	Entry Price	Target Price	Stop Loss	Exit Price

Reason for Trade Entry:
Strategy:
Trade Result Remarks:
Notes:

Trade #   Entry Date   Time Open   Time Closed

FX Pair	Buy / Sell	Trade Size	Entry Price	Target Price	Stop Loss	Exit Price

Reason for Trade Entry:
Strategy:
Trade Result Remarks:
Notes:

Trade #   Entry Date   Time Open   Time Closed

FX Pair	Buy / Sell	Trade Size	Entry Price	Target Price	Stop Loss	Exit Price

Reason for Trade Entry:
Strategy:
Trade Result Remarks:
Notes:

Trade #   Entry Date   Time Open   Time Closed

FX Pair	Buy / Sell	Trade Size	Entry Price	Target Price	Stop Loss	Exit Price

Reason for Trade Entry:
Strategy:
Trade Result Remarks:
Notes:

Trade #   Entry Date   Time Open   Time Closed

FX Pair	Buy / Sell	Trade Size	Entry Price	Target Price	Stop Loss	Exit Price

Reason for Trade Entry:
Strategy:
Trade Result Remarks:
Notes:

Trade #   Entry Date   Time Open   Time Closed

FX Pair	Buy / Sell	Trade Size	Entry Price	Target Price	Stop Loss	Exit Price

Reason for Trade Entry:
Strategy:
Trade Result Remarks:
Notes:

Trade #   **Entry Date**   **Time Open**   **Time Closed**

FX Pair	Buy / Sell	Trade Size	Entry Price	Target Price	Stop Loss	Exit Price

Reason for Trade Entry:
Strategy:
Trade Result Remarks:
Notes:

Trade #   **Entry Date**   **Time Open**   **Time Closed**

FX Pair	Buy / Sell	Trade Size	Entry Price	Target Price	Stop Loss	Exit Price

Reason for Trade Entry:
Strategy:
Trade Result Remarks:
Notes:

Trade #   Entry Date   Time Open   Time Closed

FX Pair	Buy / Sell	Trade Size	Entry Price	Target Price	Stop Loss	Exit Price

Reason for Trade Entry:
Strategy:
Trade Result Remarks:
Notes:

Trade #   Entry Date   Time Open   Time Closed

FX Pair	Buy / Sell	Trade Size	Entry Price	Target Price	Stop Loss	Exit Price

Reason for Trade Entry:
Strategy:
Trade Result Remarks:
Notes:

Trade #　　　　　　**Entry Date**　　　　　　**Time Open**　　　　　　**Time Closed**

FX Pair	Buy / Sell	Trade Size	Entry Price	Target Price	Stop Loss	Exit Price

Reason for Trade Entry:
Strategy:
Trade Result Remarks:
Notes:

Trade #　　　　　　**Entry Date**　　　　　　**Time Open**　　　　　　**Time Closed**

FX Pair	Buy / Sell	Trade Size	Entry Price	Target Price	Stop Loss	Exit Price

Reason for Trade Entry:
Strategy:
Trade Result Remarks:
Notes:

Trade #　　　　　Entry Date　　　　　Time Open　　　　　Time Closed

FX Pair	Buy / Sell	Trade Size	Entry Price	Target Price	Stop Loss	Exit Price

Reason for Trade Entry:
Strategy:
Trade Result Remarks:
Notes:

Trade #　　　　　Entry Date　　　　　Time Open　　　　　Time Closed

FX Pair	Buy / Sell	Trade Size	Entry Price	Target Price	Stop Loss	Exit Price

Reason for Trade Entry:
Strategy:
Trade Result Remarks:
Notes:

Trade #   Entry Date   Time Open   Time Closed

FX Pair	Buy / Sell	Trade Size	Entry Price	Target Price	Stop Loss	Exit Price

Reason for Trade Entry:
Strategy:
Trade Result Remarks:
Notes:

Trade #   Entry Date   Time Open   Time Closed

FX Pair	Buy / Sell	Trade Size	Entry Price	Target Price	Stop Loss	Exit Price

Reason for Trade Entry:
Strategy:
Trade Result Remarks:
Notes:

Trade #   Entry Date   Time Open   Time Closed

FX Pair	Buy / Sell	Trade Size	Entry Price	Target Price	Stop Loss	Exit Price

Reason for Trade Entry:
Strategy:
Trade Result Remarks:
Notes:

Trade #   Entry Date   Time Open   Time Closed

FX Pair	Buy / Sell	Trade Size	Entry Price	Target Price	Stop Loss	Exit Price

Reason for Trade Entry:
Strategy:
Trade Result Remarks:
Notes:

Trade #   **Entry Date**   **Time Open**   **Time Closed**

FX Pair	Buy / Sell	Trade Size	Entry Price	Target Price	Stop Loss	Exit Price

Reason for Trade Entry:
Strategy:
Trade Result Remarks:
Notes:

Trade #   **Entry Date**   **Time Open**   **Time Closed**

FX Pair	Buy / Sell	Trade Size	Entry Price	Target Price	Stop Loss	Exit Price

Reason for Trade Entry:
Strategy:
Trade Result Remarks:
Notes:

Trade #   Entry Date   Time Open   Time Closed

FX Pair	Buy / Sell	Trade Size	Entry Price	Target Price	Stop Loss	Exit Price

Reason for Trade Entry:
Strategy:
Trade Result Remarks:
Notes:

Trade #   Entry Date   Time Open   Time Closed

FX Pair	Buy / Sell	Trade Size	Entry Price	Target Price	Stop Loss	Exit Price

Reason for Trade Entry:
Strategy:
Trade Result Remarks:
Notes:

Trade #   **Entry Date**   **Time Open**   **Time Closed**

FX Pair	Buy / Sell	Trade Size	Entry Price	Target Price	Stop Loss	Exit Price

Reason for Trade Entry:
Strategy:
Trade Result Remarks:
Notes:

Trade #   **Entry Date**   **Time Open**   **Time Closed**

FX Pair	Buy / Sell	Trade Size	Entry Price	Target Price	Stop Loss	Exit Price

Reason for Trade Entry:
Strategy:
Trade Result Remarks:
Notes:

Trade #	**Entry Date**	**Time Open**	**Time Closed**

FX Pair	Buy / Sell	Trade Size	Entry Price	Target Price	Stop Loss	Exit Price

Reason for Trade Entry:
Strategy:
Trade Result Remarks:
Notes:

Trade #	**Entry Date**	**Time Open**	**Time Closed**

FX Pair	Buy / Sell	Trade Size	Entry Price	Target Price	Stop Loss	Exit Price

Reason for Trade Entry:
Strategy:
Trade Result Remarks:
Notes:

Trade #	Entry Date	Time Open	Time Closed

FX Pair	Buy / Sell	Trade Size	Entry Price	Target Price	Stop Loss	Exit Price

Reason for Trade Entry:
Strategy:
Trade Result Remarks:
Notes:

Trade #	Entry Date	Time Open	Time Closed

FX Pair	Buy / Sell	Trade Size	Entry Price	Target Price	Stop Loss	Exit Price

Reason for Trade Entry:
Strategy:
Trade Result Remarks:
Notes:

Trade #   Entry Date   Time Open   Time Closed

FX Pair	Buy / Sell	Trade Size	Entry Price	Target Price	Stop Loss	Exit Price

Reason for Trade Entry:
Strategy:
Trade Result Remarks:
Notes:

Trade #   Entry Date   Time Open   Time Closed

FX Pair	Buy / Sell	Trade Size	Entry Price	Target Price	Stop Loss	Exit Price

Reason for Trade Entry:
Strategy:
Trade Result Remarks:
Notes:

Trade #   **Entry Date**   **Time Open**   **Time Closed**

FX Pair	Buy / Sell	Trade Size	Entry Price	Target Price	Stop Loss	Exit Price

Reason for Trade Entry:
Strategy:
Trade Result Remarks:
Notes:

Trade #   **Entry Date**   **Time Open**   **Time Closed**

FX Pair	Buy / Sell	Trade Size	Entry Price	Target Price	Stop Loss	Exit Price

Reason for Trade Entry:
Strategy:
Trade Result Remarks:
Notes:

Trade #   Entry Date   Time Open   Time Closed

FX Pair	Buy / Sell	Trade Size	Entry Price	Target Price	Stop Loss	Exit Price

Reason for Trade Entry:
Strategy:
Trade Result Remarks:
Notes:

Trade #   Entry Date   Time Open   Time Closed

FX Pair	Buy / Sell	Trade Size	Entry Price	Target Price	Stop Loss	Exit Price

Reason for Trade Entry:
Strategy:
Trade Result Remarks:
Notes:

Trade #   Entry Date   Time Open   Time Closed

FX Pair	Buy / Sell	Trade Size	Entry Price	Target Price	Stop Loss	Exit Price

Reason for Trade Entry:
Strategy:
Trade Result Remarks:
Notes:

Trade #   Entry Date   Time Open   Time Closed

FX Pair	Buy / Sell	Trade Size	Entry Price	Target Price	Stop Loss	Exit Price

Reason for Trade Entry:
Strategy:
Trade Result Remarks:
Notes:

Trade #   Entry Date   Time Open   Time Closed

FX Pair	Buy / Sell	Trade Size	Entry Price	Target Price	Stop Loss	Exit Price

Reason for Trade Entry:
Strategy:
Trade Result Remarks:
Notes:

Trade #   Entry Date   Time Open   Time Closed

FX Pair	Buy / Sell	Trade Size	Entry Price	Target Price	Stop Loss	Exit Price

Reason for Trade Entry:
Strategy:
Trade Result Remarks:
Notes:

Trade #	Entry Date	Time Open	Time Closed

FX Pair	Buy / Sell	Trade Size	Entry Price	Target Price	Stop Loss	Exit Price

Reason for Trade Entry:
Strategy:
Trade Result Remarks:
Notes:

Trade #	Entry Date	Time Open	Time Closed

FX Pair	Buy / Sell	Trade Size	Entry Price	Target Price	Stop Loss	Exit Price

Reason for Trade Entry:
Strategy:
Trade Result Remarks:
Notes:

Trade #　　　　　　Entry Date　　　　　　Time Open　　　　　　Time Closed

FX Pair	Buy / Sell	Trade Size	Entry Price	Target Price	Stop Loss	Exit Price

Reason for Trade Entry:
Strategy:
Trade Result Remarks:
Notes:

Trade #　　　　　　Entry Date　　　　　　Time Open　　　　　　Time Closed

FX Pair	Buy / Sell	Trade Size	Entry Price	Target Price	Stop Loss	Exit Price

Reason for Trade Entry:
Strategy:
Trade Result Remarks:
Notes:

Trade #　　　　　Entry Date　　　　　Time Open　　　　　Time Closed

FX Pair	Buy / Sell	Trade Size	Entry Price	Target Price	Stop Loss	Exit Price

Reason for Trade Entry:
Strategy:
Trade Result Remarks:
Notes:

Trade #　　　　　Entry Date　　　　　Time Open　　　　　Time Closed

FX Pair	Buy / Sell	Trade Size	Entry Price	Target Price	Stop Loss	Exit Price

Reason for Trade Entry:
Strategy:
Trade Result Remarks:
Notes:

Trade #   **Entry Date**   **Time Open**   **Time Closed**

FX Pair	Buy / Sell	Trade Size	Entry Price	Target Price	Stop Loss	Exit Price

Reason for Trade Entry:
Strategy:
Trade Result Remarks:
Notes:

Trade #   **Entry Date**   **Time Open**   **Time Closed**

FX Pair	Buy / Sell	Trade Size	Entry Price	Target Price	Stop Loss	Exit Price

Reason for Trade Entry:
Strategy:
Trade Result Remarks:
Notes:

Trade #   Entry Date   Time Open   Time Closed

FX Pair	Buy / Sell	Trade Size	Entry Price	Target Price	Stop Loss	Exit Price

Reason for Trade Entry:
Strategy:
Trade Result Remarks:
Notes:

Trade #   Entry Date   Time Open   Time Closed

FX Pair	Buy / Sell	Trade Size	Entry Price	Target Price	Stop Loss	Exit Price

Reason for Trade Entry:
Strategy:
Trade Result Remarks:
Notes:

Trade #   Entry Date   Time Open   Time Closed

FX Pair	Buy / Sell	Trade Size	Entry Price	Target Price	Stop Loss	Exit Price

Reason for Trade Entry:
Strategy:
Trade Result Remarks:
Notes:

Trade #   Entry Date   Time Open   Time Closed

FX Pair	Buy / Sell	Trade Size	Entry Price	Target Price	Stop Loss	Exit Price

Reason for Trade Entry:
Strategy:
Trade Result Remarks:
Notes:

Trade #　　　　　**Entry Date**　　　　　**Time Open**　　　　　**Time Closed**

FX Pair	Buy / Sell	Trade Size	Entry Price	Target Price	Stop Loss	Exit Price

Reason for Trade Entry:
Strategy:
Trade Result Remarks:
Notes:

Trade #　　　　　**Entry Date**　　　　　**Time Open**　　　　　**Time Closed**

FX Pair	Buy / Sell	Trade Size	Entry Price	Target Price	Stop Loss	Exit Price

Reason for Trade Entry:
Strategy:
Trade Result Remarks:
Notes:

Trade #   Entry Date   Time Open   Time Closed

FX Pair	Buy / Sell	Trade Size	Entry Price	Target Price	Stop Loss	Exit Price

Reason for Trade Entry:
Strategy:
Trade Result Remarks:
Notes:

Trade #   Entry Date   Time Open   Time Closed

FX Pair	Buy / Sell	Trade Size	Entry Price	Target Price	Stop Loss	Exit Price

Reason for Trade Entry:
Strategy:
Trade Result Remarks:
Notes:

Trade # **Entry Date** **Time Open** **Time Closed**

FX Pair	Buy / Sell	Trade Size	Entry Price	Target Price	Stop Loss	Exit Price

Reason for Trade Entry:
Strategy:
Trade Result Remarks:
Notes:

Trade # **Entry Date** **Time Open** **Time Closed**

FX Pair	Buy / Sell	Trade Size	Entry Price	Target Price	Stop Loss	Exit Price

Reason for Trade Entry:
Strategy:
Trade Result Remarks:
Notes:

Trade #   Entry Date   Time Open   Time Closed

FX Pair	Buy / Sell	Trade Size	Entry Price	Target Price	Stop Loss	Exit Price

Reason for Trade Entry:
Strategy:
Trade Result Remarks:
Notes:

Trade #   Entry Date   Time Open   Time Closed

FX Pair	Buy / Sell	Trade Size	Entry Price	Target Price	Stop Loss	Exit Price

Reason for Trade Entry:
Strategy:
Trade Result Remarks:
Notes:

Trade #   Entry Date   Time Open   Time Closed

FX Pair	Buy / Sell	Trade Size	Entry Price	Target Price	Stop Loss	Exit Price

Reason for Trade Entry:
Strategy:
Trade Result Remarks:
Notes:

Trade #   Entry Date   Time Open   Time Closed

FX Pair	Buy / Sell	Trade Size	Entry Price	Target Price	Stop Loss	Exit Price

Reason for Trade Entry:
Strategy:
Trade Result Remarks:
Notes:

Trade #	Entry Date	Time Open	Time Closed

FX Pair	Buy / Sell	Trade Size	Entry Price	Target Price	Stop Loss	Exit Price

Reason for Trade Entry:
Strategy:
Trade Result Remarks:
Notes:

Trade #	Entry Date	Time Open	Time Closed

FX Pair	Buy / Sell	Trade Size	Entry Price	Target Price	Stop Loss	Exit Price

Reason for Trade Entry:
Strategy:
Trade Result Remarks:
Notes:

Trade #   Entry Date   Time Open   Time Closed

FX Pair	Buy / Sell	Trade Size	Entry Price	Target Price	Stop Loss	Exit Price

Reason for Trade Entry:
Strategy:
Trade Result Remarks:
Notes:

Trade #   Entry Date   Time Open   Time Closed

FX Pair	Buy / Sell	Trade Size	Entry Price	Target Price	Stop Loss	Exit Price

Reason for Trade Entry:
Strategy:
Trade Result Remarks:
Notes:

Trade #   Entry Date   Time Open   Time Closed

FX Pair	Buy / Sell	Trade Size	Entry Price	Target Price	Stop Loss	Exit Price

Reason for Trade Entry:
Strategy:
Trade Result Remarks:
Notes:

Trade #   Entry Date   Time Open   Time Closed

FX Pair	Buy / Sell	Trade Size	Entry Price	Target Price	Stop Loss	Exit Price

Reason for Trade Entry:
Strategy:
Trade Result Remarks:
Notes:

Trade #   Entry Date   Time Open   Time Closed

FX Pair	Buy / Sell	Trade Size	Entry Price	Target Price	Stop Loss	Exit Price

Reason for Trade Entry:
Strategy:
Trade Result Remarks:
Notes:

Trade #   Entry Date   Time Open   Time Closed

FX Pair	Buy / Sell	Trade Size	Entry Price	Target Price	Stop Loss	Exit Price

Reason for Trade Entry:
Strategy:
Trade Result Remarks:
Notes:

Trade #   Entry Date   Time Open   Time Closed

FX Pair	Buy / Sell	Trade Size	Entry Price	Target Price	Stop Loss	Exit Price

Reason for Trade Entry:
Strategy:
Trade Result Remarks:
Notes:

Trade #   Entry Date   Time Open   Time Closed

FX Pair	Buy / Sell	Trade Size	Entry Price	Target Price	Stop Loss	Exit Price

Reason for Trade Entry:
Strategy:
Trade Result Remarks:
Notes:

Trade #　　　　　　Entry Date　　　　　　Time Open　　　　　　Time Closed

FX Pair	Buy / Sell	Trade Size	Entry Price	Target Price	Stop Loss	Exit Price

Reason for Trade Entry:
Strategy:
Trade Result Remarks:
Notes:

Trade #　　　　　　Entry Date　　　　　　Time Open　　　　　　Time Closed

FX Pair	Buy / Sell	Trade Size	Entry Price	Target Price	Stop Loss	Exit Price

Reason for Trade Entry:
Strategy:
Trade Result Remarks:
Notes:

Trade #   Entry Date   Time Open   Time Closed

FX Pair	Buy / Sell	Trade Size	Entry Price	Target Price	Stop Loss	Exit Price

Reason for Trade Entry:
Strategy:
Trade Result Remarks:
Notes:

Trade #   Entry Date   Time Open   Time Closed

FX Pair	Buy / Sell	Trade Size	Entry Price	Target Price	Stop Loss	Exit Price

Reason for Trade Entry:
Strategy:
Trade Result Remarks:
Notes:

Trade #   **Entry Date**   **Time Open**   **Time Closed**

FX Pair	Buy / Sell	Trade Size	Entry Price	Target Price	Stop Loss	Exit Price

Reason for Trade Entry:
Strategy:
Trade Result Remarks:
Notes:

Trade #   **Entry Date**   **Time Open**   **Time Closed**

FX Pair	Buy / Sell	Trade Size	Entry Price	Target Price	Stop Loss	Exit Price

Reason for Trade Entry:
Strategy:
Trade Result Remarks:
Notes:

Trade #   **Entry Date**   **Time Open**   **Time Closed**

FX Pair	Buy / Sell	Trade Size	Entry Price	Target Price	Stop Loss	Exit Price

Reason for Trade Entry:
Strategy:
Trade Result Remarks:
Notes:

Trade #   **Entry Date**   **Time Open**   **Time Closed**

FX Pair	Buy / Sell	Trade Size	Entry Price	Target Price	Stop Loss	Exit Price

Reason for Trade Entry:
Strategy:
Trade Result Remarks:
Notes:

Trade #　　　　　　　Entry Date　　　　　　　Time Open　　　　　　　Time Closed

FX Pair	Buy / Sell	Trade Size	Entry Price	Target Price	Stop Loss	Exit Price

Reason for Trade Entry:
Strategy:
Trade Result Remarks:
Notes:

Trade #　　　　　　　Entry Date　　　　　　　Time Open　　　　　　　Time Closed

FX Pair	Buy / Sell	Trade Size	Entry Price	Target Price	Stop Loss	Exit Price

Reason for Trade Entry:
Strategy:
Trade Result Remarks:
Notes:

Trade #   Entry Date   Time Open   Time Closed

FX Pair	Buy / Sell	Trade Size	Entry Price	Target Price	Stop Loss	Exit Price

Reason for Trade Entry:
Strategy:
Trade Result Remarks:
Notes:

Trade #   Entry Date   Time Open   Time Closed

FX Pair	Buy / Sell	Trade Size	Entry Price	Target Price	Stop Loss	Exit Price

Reason for Trade Entry:
Strategy:
Trade Result Remarks:
Notes:

Trade #   Entry Date   Time Open   Time Closed

FX Pair	Buy / Sell	Trade Size	Entry Price	Target Price	Stop Loss	Exit Price

Reason for Trade Entry:
Strategy:
Trade Result Remarks:
Notes:

Trade #   Entry Date   Time Open   Time Closed

FX Pair	Buy / Sell	Trade Size	Entry Price	Target Price	Stop Loss	Exit Price

Reason for Trade Entry:
Strategy:
Trade Result Remarks:
Notes:

Trade #   Entry Date   Time Open   Time Closed

FX Pair	Buy / Sell	Trade Size	Entry Price	Target Price	Stop Loss	Exit Price

Reason for Trade Entry:
Strategy:
Trade Result Remarks:
Notes:

Trade #   Entry Date   Time Open   Time Closed

FX Pair	Buy / Sell	Trade Size	Entry Price	Target Price	Stop Loss	Exit Price

Reason for Trade Entry:
Strategy:
Trade Result Remarks:
Notes:

Trade #   Entry Date   Time Open   Time Closed

FX Pair	Buy / Sell	Trade Size	Entry Price	Target Price	Stop Loss	Exit Price

Reason for Trade Entry:
Strategy:
Trade Result Remarks:
Notes:

Trade #   Entry Date   Time Open   Time Closed

FX Pair	Buy / Sell	Trade Size	Entry Price	Target Price	Stop Loss	Exit Price

Reason for Trade Entry:
Strategy:
Trade Result Remarks:
Notes:

Trade #	Entry Date	Time Open	Time Closed

FX Pair	Buy / Sell	Trade Size	Entry Price	Target Price	Stop Loss	Exit Price

Reason for Trade Entry:
Strategy:
Trade Result Remarks:
Notes:

Trade #	Entry Date	Time Open	Time Closed

FX Pair	Buy / Sell	Trade Size	Entry Price	Target Price	Stop Loss	Exit Price

Reason for Trade Entry:
Strategy:
Trade Result Remarks:
Notes:

Trade #　　　　　　**Entry Date**　　　　　　**Time Open**　　　　　　**Time Closed**

FX Pair	Buy / Sell	Trade Size	Entry Price	Target Price	Stop Loss	Exit Price

Reason for Trade Entry:
Strategy:
Trade Result Remarks:
Notes:

Trade #　　　　　　**Entry Date**　　　　　　**Time Open**　　　　　　**Time Closed**

FX Pair	Buy / Sell	Trade Size	Entry Price	Target Price	Stop Loss	Exit Price

Reason for Trade Entry:
Strategy:
Trade Result Remarks:
Notes:

Trade #   Entry Date   Time Open   Time Closed

FX Pair	Buy / Sell	Trade Size	Entry Price	Target Price	Stop Loss	Exit Price

Reason for Trade Entry:
Strategy:
Trade Result Remarks:
Notes:

Trade #   Entry Date   Time Open   Time Closed

FX Pair	Buy / Sell	Trade Size	Entry Price	Target Price	Stop Loss	Exit Price

Reason for Trade Entry:
Strategy:
Trade Result Remarks:
Notes:

Trade #　　　　　　　Entry Date　　　　　　　Time Open　　　　　　　Time Closed

FX Pair	Buy / Sell	Trade Size	Entry Price	Target Price	Stop Loss	Exit Price

Reason for Trade Entry:
Strategy:
Trade Result Remarks:
Notes:

Trade #　　　　　　　Entry Date　　　　　　　Time Open　　　　　　　Time Closed

FX Pair	Buy / Sell	Trade Size	Entry Price	Target Price	Stop Loss	Exit Price

Reason for Trade Entry:
Strategy:
Trade Result Remarks:
Notes:

Trade #   **Entry Date**   **Time Open**   **Time Closed**

FX Pair	Buy / Sell	Trade Size	Entry Price	Target Price	Stop Loss	Exit Price

Reason for Trade Entry:
Strategy:
Trade Result Remarks:
Notes:

Trade #   **Entry Date**   **Time Open**   **Time Closed**

FX Pair	Buy / Sell	Trade Size	Entry Price	Target Price	Stop Loss	Exit Price

Reason for Trade Entry:
Strategy:
Trade Result Remarks:
Notes:

Trade #   Entry Date   Time Open   Time Closed

FX Pair	Buy / Sell	Trade Size	Entry Price	Target Price	Stop Loss	Exit Price

Reason for Trade Entry:
Strategy:
Trade Result Remarks:
Notes:

Trade #   Entry Date   Time Open   Time Closed

FX Pair	Buy / Sell	Trade Size	Entry Price	Target Price	Stop Loss	Exit Price

Reason for Trade Entry:
Strategy:
Trade Result Remarks:
Notes:

Trade #   Entry Date   Time Open   Time Closed

FX Pair	Buy / Sell	Trade Size	Entry Price	Target Price	Stop Loss	Exit Price

Reason for Trade Entry:
Strategy:
Trade Result Remarks:
Notes:

Trade #   Entry Date   Time Open   Time Closed

FX Pair	Buy / Sell	Trade Size	Entry Price	Target Price	Stop Loss	Exit Price

Reason for Trade Entry:
Strategy:
Trade Result Remarks:
Notes:

Trade #   **Entry Date**   **Time Open**   **Time Closed**

FX Pair	Buy / Sell	Trade Size	Entry Price	Target Price	Stop Loss	Exit Price

Reason for Trade Entry:
Strategy:
Trade Result Remarks:
Notes:

Trade #   **Entry Date**   **Time Open**   **Time Closed**

FX Pair	Buy / Sell	Trade Size	Entry Price	Target Price	Stop Loss	Exit Price

Reason for Trade Entry:
Strategy:
Trade Result Remarks:
Notes:

Trade # **Entry Date** **Time Open** **Time Closed**

FX Pair	Buy / Sell	Trade Size	Entry Price	Target Price	Stop Loss	Exit Price

Reason for Trade Entry:
Strategy:
Trade Result Remarks:
Notes:

Trade # **Entry Date** **Time Open** **Time Closed**

FX Pair	Buy / Sell	Trade Size	Entry Price	Target Price	Stop Loss	Exit Price

Reason for Trade Entry:
Strategy:
Trade Result Remarks:
Notes:

Trade #   Entry Date   Time Open   Time Closed

FX Pair	Buy / Sell	Trade Size	Entry Price	Target Price	Stop Loss	Exit Price

Reason for Trade Entry:
Strategy:
Trade Result Remarks:
Notes:

Trade #   Entry Date   Time Open   Time Closed

FX Pair	Buy / Sell	Trade Size	Entry Price	Target Price	Stop Loss	Exit Price

Reason for Trade Entry:
Strategy:
Trade Result Remarks:
Notes:

Trade #   Entry Date   Time Open   Time Closed

FX Pair	Buy / Sell	Trade Size	Entry Price	Target Price	Stop Loss	Exit Price

Reason for Trade Entry:
Strategy:
Trade Result Remarks:
Notes:

Trade #   Entry Date   Time Open   Time Closed

FX Pair	Buy / Sell	Trade Size	Entry Price	Target Price	Stop Loss	Exit Price

Reason for Trade Entry:
Strategy:
Trade Result Remarks:
Notes:

Trade #   Entry Date   Time Open   Time Closed

FX Pair	Buy / Sell	Trade Size	Entry Price	Target Price	Stop Loss	Exit Price

Reason for Trade Entry:
Strategy:
Trade Result Remarks:
Notes:

Trade #   Entry Date   Time Open   Time Closed

FX Pair	Buy / Sell	Trade Size	Entry Price	Target Price	Stop Loss	Exit Price

Reason for Trade Entry:
Strategy:
Trade Result Remarks:
Notes:

Trade #   Entry Date   Time Open   Time Closed

FX Pair	Buy / Sell	Trade Size	Entry Price	Target Price	Stop Loss	Exit Price

Reason for Trade Entry:
Strategy:
Trade Result Remarks:
Notes:

Trade #   Entry Date   Time Open   Time Closed

FX Pair	Buy / Sell	Trade Size	Entry Price	Target Price	Stop Loss	Exit Price

Reason for Trade Entry:
Strategy:
Trade Result Remarks:
Notes:

Trade #　　　　　**Entry Date**　　　　　**Time Open**　　　　　**Time Closed**

FX Pair	Buy / Sell	Trade Size	Entry Price	Target Price	Stop Loss	Exit Price

Reason for Trade Entry:
Strategy:
Trade Result Remarks:
Notes:

Trade #　　　　　**Entry Date**　　　　　**Time Open**　　　　　**Time Closed**

FX Pair	Buy / Sell	Trade Size	Entry Price	Target Price	Stop Loss	Exit Price

Reason for Trade Entry:
Strategy:
Trade Result Remarks:
Notes:

Trade #   Entry Date   Time Open   Time Closed

FX Pair	Buy / Sell	Trade Size	Entry Price	Target Price	Stop Loss	Exit Price

Reason for Trade Entry:
Strategy:
Trade Result Remarks:
Notes:

Trade #   Entry Date   Time Open   Time Closed

FX Pair	Buy / Sell	Trade Size	Entry Price	Target Price	Stop Loss	Exit Price

Reason for Trade Entry:
Strategy:
Trade Result Remarks:
Notes:

Trade #   Entry Date   Time Open   Time Closed

FX Pair	Buy / Sell	Trade Size	Entry Price	Target Price	Stop Loss	Exit Price

Reason for Trade Entry:
Strategy:
Trade Result Remarks:
Notes:

Trade #   Entry Date   Time Open   Time Closed

FX Pair	Buy / Sell	Trade Size	Entry Price	Target Price	Stop Loss	Exit Price

Reason for Trade Entry:
Strategy:
Trade Result Remarks:
Notes:

Trade #　　　　　**Entry Date**　　　　　**Time Open**　　　　　**Time Closed**

FX Pair	Buy / Sell	Trade Size	Entry Price	Target Price	Stop Loss	Exit Price

Reason for Trade Entry:
Strategy:
Trade Result Remarks:
Notes:

Trade #　　　　　**Entry Date**　　　　　**Time Open**　　　　　**Time Closed**

FX Pair	Buy / Sell	Trade Size	Entry Price	Target Price	Stop Loss	Exit Price

Reason for Trade Entry:
Strategy:
Trade Result Remarks:
Notes:

Trade #   Entry Date   Time Open   Time Closed

FX Pair	Buy / Sell	Trade Size	Entry Price	Target Price	Stop Loss	Exit Price

Reason for Trade Entry:
Strategy:
Trade Result Remarks:
Notes:

Trade #   Entry Date   Time Open   Time Closed

FX Pair	Buy / Sell	Trade Size	Entry Price	Target Price	Stop Loss	Exit Price

Reason for Trade Entry:
Strategy:
Trade Result Remarks:
Notes:

Trade #   Entry Date   Time Open   Time Closed

FX Pair	Buy / Sell	Trade Size	Entry Price	Target Price	Stop Loss	Exit Price

Reason for Trade Entry:
Strategy:
Trade Result Remarks:
Notes:

Trade #   Entry Date   Time Open   Time Closed

FX Pair	Buy / Sell	Trade Size	Entry Price	Target Price	Stop Loss	Exit Price

Reason for Trade Entry:
Strategy:
Trade Result Remarks:
Notes:

Trade #   Entry Date   Time Open   Time Closed

FX Pair	Buy / Sell	Trade Size	Entry Price	Target Price	Stop Loss	Exit Price

Reason for Trade Entry:
Strategy:
Trade Result Remarks:
Notes:

Trade #   Entry Date   Time Open   Time Closed

FX Pair	Buy / Sell	Trade Size	Entry Price	Target Price	Stop Loss	Exit Price

Reason for Trade Entry:
Strategy:
Trade Result Remarks:
Notes:

Trade #   Entry Date   Time Open   Time Closed

FX Pair	Buy / Sell	Trade Size	Entry Price	Target Price	Stop Loss	Exit Price

Reason for Trade Entry:
Strategy:
Trade Result Remarks:
Notes:

Trade #   Entry Date   Time Open   Time Closed

FX Pair	Buy / Sell	Trade Size	Entry Price	Target Price	Stop Loss	Exit Price

Reason for Trade Entry:
Strategy:
Trade Result Remarks:
Notes:

Trade #   Entry Date   Time Open   Time Closed

FX Pair	Buy / Sell	Trade Size	Entry Price	Target Price	Stop Loss	Exit Price

Reason for Trade Entry:
Strategy:
Trade Result Remarks:
Notes:

Trade #   Entry Date   Time Open   Time Closed

FX Pair	Buy / Sell	Trade Size	Entry Price	Target Price	Stop Loss	Exit Price

Reason for Trade Entry:
Strategy:
Trade Result Remarks:
Notes:

Trade #   Entry Date   Time Open   Time Closed

FX Pair	Buy / Sell	Trade Size	Entry Price	Target Price	Stop Loss	Exit Price

Reason for Trade Entry:
Strategy:
Trade Result Remarks:
Notes:

Trade #   Entry Date   Time Open   Time Closed

FX Pair	Buy / Sell	Trade Size	Entry Price	Target Price	Stop Loss	Exit Price

Reason for Trade Entry:
Strategy:
Trade Result Remarks:
Notes:

Trade #   Entry Date   Time Open   Time Closed

FX Pair	Buy / Sell	Trade Size	Entry Price	Target Price	Stop Loss	Exit Price

Reason for Trade Entry:
Strategy:
Trade Result Remarks:
Notes:

Trade #   Entry Date   Time Open   Time Closed

FX Pair	Buy / Sell	Trade Size	Entry Price	Target Price	Stop Loss	Exit Price

Reason for Trade Entry:
Strategy:
Trade Result Remarks:
Notes:

Trade # Entry Date Time Open Time Closed

FX Pair	Buy / Sell	Trade Size	Entry Price	Target Price	Stop Loss	Exit Price

Reason for Trade Entry:
Strategy:
Trade Result Remarks:
Notes:

Trade # Entry Date Time Open Time Closed

FX Pair	Buy / Sell	Trade Size	Entry Price	Target Price	Stop Loss	Exit Price

Reason for Trade Entry:
Strategy:
Trade Result Remarks:
Notes:

Trade #   Entry Date   Time Open   Time Closed

FX Pair	Buy / Sell	Trade Size	Entry Price	Target Price	Stop Loss	Exit Price

Reason for Trade Entry:
Strategy:
Trade Result Remarks:
Notes:

Trade #   Entry Date   Time Open   Time Closed

FX Pair	Buy / Sell	Trade Size	Entry Price	Target Price	Stop Loss	Exit Price

Reason for Trade Entry:
Strategy:
Trade Result Remarks:
Notes:

Trade #   Entry Date   Time Open   Time Closed

FX Pair	Buy / Sell	Trade Size	Entry Price	Target Price	Stop Loss	Exit Price

Reason for Trade Entry:
Strategy:
Trade Result Remarks:
Notes:

Trade #   Entry Date   Time Open   Time Closed

FX Pair	Buy / Sell	Trade Size	Entry Price	Target Price	Stop Loss	Exit Price

Reason for Trade Entry:
Strategy:
Trade Result Remarks:
Notes:

Trade #   **Entry Date**   **Time Open**   **Time Closed**

FX Pair	Buy / Sell	Trade Size	Entry Price	Target Price	Stop Loss	Exit Price

Reason for Trade Entry:
Strategy:
Trade Result Remarks:
Notes:

Trade #   **Entry Date**   **Time Open**   **Time Closed**

FX Pair	Buy / Sell	Trade Size	Entry Price	Target Price	Stop Loss	Exit Price

Reason for Trade Entry:
Strategy:
Trade Result Remarks:
Notes:

Trade #   **Entry Date**   **Time Open**   **Time Closed**

FX Pair	Buy / Sell	Trade Size	Entry Price	Target Price	Stop Loss	Exit Price

Reason for Trade Entry:
Strategy:
Trade Result Remarks:
Notes:

Trade #   **Entry Date**   **Time Open**   **Time Closed**

FX Pair	Buy / Sell	Trade Size	Entry Price	Target Price	Stop Loss	Exit Price

Reason for Trade Entry:
Strategy:
Trade Result Remarks:
Notes:

Trade #   Entry Date   Time Open   Time Closed

FX Pair	Buy / Sell	Trade Size	Entry Price	Target Price	Stop Loss	Exit Price

Reason for Trade Entry:
Strategy:
Trade Result Remarks:
Notes:

Trade #   Entry Date   Time Open   Time Closed

FX Pair	Buy / Sell	Trade Size	Entry Price	Target Price	Stop Loss	Exit Price

Reason for Trade Entry:
Strategy:
Trade Result Remarks:
Notes:

Trade #   Entry Date   Time Open   Time Closed

FX Pair	Buy / Sell	Trade Size	Entry Price	Target Price	Stop Loss	Exit Price

Reason for Trade Entry:
Strategy:
Trade Result Remarks:
Notes:

Trade #   Entry Date   Time Open   Time Closed

FX Pair	Buy / Sell	Trade Size	Entry Price	Target Price	Stop Loss	Exit Price

Reason for Trade Entry:
Strategy:
Trade Result Remarks:
Notes:

Trade #	Entry Date	Time Open	Time Closed

FX Pair	Buy / Sell	Trade Size	Entry Price	Target Price	Stop Loss	Exit Price

Reason for Trade Entry:
Strategy:
Trade Result Remarks:
Notes:

Trade #	Entry Date	Time Open	Time Closed

FX Pair	Buy / Sell	Trade Size	Entry Price	Target Price	Stop Loss	Exit Price

Reason for Trade Entry:
Strategy:
Trade Result Remarks:
Notes:

Trade #   Entry Date   Time Open   Time Closed

FX Pair	Buy / Sell	Trade Size	Entry Price	Target Price	Stop Loss	Exit Price

Reason for Trade Entry:
Strategy:
Trade Result Remarks:
Notes:

Trade #   Entry Date   Time Open   Time Closed

FX Pair	Buy / Sell	Trade Size	Entry Price	Target Price	Stop Loss	Exit Price

Reason for Trade Entry:
Strategy:
Trade Result Remarks:
Notes:

Trade #   Entry Date   Time Open   Time Closed

FX Pair	Buy / Sell	Trade Size	Entry Price	Target Price	Stop Loss	Exit Price

Reason for Trade Entry:
Strategy:
Trade Result Remarks:
Notes:

Trade #   Entry Date   Time Open   Time Closed

FX Pair	Buy / Sell	Trade Size	Entry Price	Target Price	Stop Loss	Exit Price

Reason for Trade Entry:
Strategy:
Trade Result Remarks:
Notes:

Trade #   Entry Date   Time Open   Time Closed

FX Pair	Buy / Sell	Trade Size	Entry Price	Target Price	Stop Loss	Exit Price

Reason for Trade Entry:
Strategy:
Trade Result Remarks:
Notes:

Trade #   Entry Date   Time Open   Time Closed

FX Pair	Buy / Sell	Trade Size	Entry Price	Target Price	Stop Loss	Exit Price

Reason for Trade Entry:
Strategy:
Trade Result Remarks:
Notes:

Trade #　　　　　Entry Date　　　　　Time Open　　　　　Time Closed

FX Pair	Buy / Sell	Trade Size	Entry Price	Target Price	Stop Loss	Exit Price

Reason for Trade Entry:
Strategy:
Trade Result Remarks:
Notes:

Trade #　　　　　Entry Date　　　　　Time Open　　　　　Time Closed

FX Pair	Buy / Sell	Trade Size	Entry Price	Target Price	Stop Loss	Exit Price

Reason for Trade Entry:
Strategy:
Trade Result Remarks:
Notes:

Trade #　　　　　**Entry Date**　　　　　**Time Open**　　　　　**Time Closed**

FX Pair	Buy / Sell	Trade Size	Entry Price	Target Price	Stop Loss	Exit Price

Reason for Trade Entry:
Strategy:
Trade Result Remarks:
Notes:

Trade #　　　　　**Entry Date**　　　　　**Time Open**　　　　　**Time Closed**

FX Pair	Buy / Sell	Trade Size	Entry Price	Target Price	Stop Loss	Exit Price

Reason for Trade Entry:
Strategy:
Trade Result Remarks:
Notes:

Trade #   Entry Date   Time Open   Time Closed

FX Pair	Buy / Sell	Trade Size	Entry Price	Target Price	Stop Loss	Exit Price

Reason for Trade Entry:
Strategy:
Trade Result Remarks:
Notes:

Trade #   Entry Date   Time Open   Time Closed

FX Pair	Buy / Sell	Trade Size	Entry Price	Target Price	Stop Loss	Exit Price

Reason for Trade Entry:
Strategy:
Trade Result Remarks:
Notes:

Trade #   Entry Date   Time Open   Time Closed

FX Pair	Buy / Sell	Trade Size	Entry Price	Target Price	Stop Loss	Exit Price

Reason for Trade Entry:
Strategy:
Trade Result Remarks:
Notes:

Trade #   Entry Date   Time Open   Time Closed

FX Pair	Buy / Sell	Trade Size	Entry Price	Target Price	Stop Loss	Exit Price

Reason for Trade Entry:
Strategy:
Trade Result Remarks:
Notes:

Trade #   Entry Date   Time Open   Time Closed

FX Pair	Buy / Sell	Trade Size	Entry Price	Target Price	Stop Loss	Exit Price

Reason for Trade Entry:
Strategy:
Trade Result Remarks:
Notes:

Trade #   Entry Date   Time Open   Time Closed

FX Pair	Buy / Sell	Trade Size	Entry Price	Target Price	Stop Loss	Exit Price

Reason for Trade Entry:
Strategy:
Trade Result Remarks:
Notes:

Trade #　　　　　　Entry Date　　　　　　Time Open　　　　　　Time Closed

FX Pair	Buy / Sell	Trade Size	Entry Price	Target Price	Stop Loss	Exit Price

Reason for Trade Entry:
Strategy:
Trade Result Remarks:
Notes:

Trade #　　　　　　Entry Date　　　　　　Time Open　　　　　　Time Closed

FX Pair	Buy / Sell	Trade Size	Entry Price	Target Price	Stop Loss	Exit Price

Reason for Trade Entry:
Strategy:
Trade Result Remarks:
Notes:

Trade # **Entry Date** **Time Open** **Time Closed**

FX Pair	Buy / Sell	Trade Size	Entry Price	Target Price	Stop Loss	Exit Price

Reason for Trade Entry:
Strategy:
Trade Result Remarks:
Notes:

Trade # **Entry Date** **Time Open** **Time Closed**

FX Pair	Buy / Sell	Trade Size	Entry Price	Target Price	Stop Loss	Exit Price

Reason for Trade Entry:
Strategy:
Trade Result Remarks:
Notes:

Trade #   Entry Date   Time Open   Time Closed

FX Pair	Buy / Sell	Trade Size	Entry Price	Target Price	Stop Loss	Exit Price

Reason for Trade Entry:
Strategy:
Trade Result Remarks:
Notes:

Trade #   Entry Date   Time Open   Time Closed

FX Pair	Buy / Sell	Trade Size	Entry Price	Target Price	Stop Loss	Exit Price

Reason for Trade Entry:
Strategy:
Trade Result Remarks:
Notes:

Trade #   Entry Date   Time Open   Time Closed

FX Pair	Buy / Sell	Trade Size	Entry Price	Target Price	Stop Loss	Exit Price

Reason for Trade Entry:
Strategy:
Trade Result Remarks:
Notes:

Trade #   Entry Date   Time Open   Time Closed

FX Pair	Buy / Sell	Trade Size	Entry Price	Target Price	Stop Loss	Exit Price

Reason for Trade Entry:
Strategy:
Trade Result Remarks:
Notes:

Trade #   **Entry Date**   **Time Open**   **Time Closed**

FX Pair	Buy / Sell	Trade Size	Entry Price	Target Price	Stop Loss	Exit Price

Reason for Trade Entry:
Strategy:
Trade Result Remarks:
Notes:

Trade #   **Entry Date**   **Time Open**   **Time Closed**

FX Pair	Buy / Sell	Trade Size	Entry Price	Target Price	Stop Loss	Exit Price

Reason for Trade Entry:
Strategy:
Trade Result Remarks:
Notes: